MW00745187

The Vision Of
HABAKKUK

The Law of Attraction in the Holy Bible

Trisha
The Law of Attraction
is a gift that keeps
on giving.

Mandy Lender, MD
2013-

The Vision Of
HABAKKUK

The Law of Attraction in the Holy Bible

Mandy (Menahem) Lender

Intermedia Publishing Group

The Vision of Habakkuk

Published by:
Intermedia Publishing Group, Inc.
P.O. Box 2825
Peoria, Arizona 85380
www.intermedia pub.com

ISBN 978-1-935529-98-9

Disclaimer: Nothing written in this book should or may possibly be interpreted or construed as a medical advice. It is strongly recommended to every reader to consult his or her licensed medical practitioner in their place of residence if they need medical advice or treatment.

To Minna Rozen

www.minnarozen.com

CONTENTS

For as he thinketh in his heart, so is he.

Proverbs 23:7

FOREWORD

In using the Holy Bible as a source for The Law of Attraction (LOA) principle, Mandy Lender presents to us a simple approach to creating results. The reader will be able to prove their truth by acting on it without fear or hesitation.

In this book, *The Vision of Habakkuk*, Mandy has simplified the LOA using biblical tenets. It has been my experience that many people resist reading the Bible for different reasons. However, the Bible is a treasury of human experience, wisdom and common sense. It is the first time that the Holy Bible is used as a platform to explain the LOA.

As thinkers we are co-creators of our life. A key concept in this book is having a vision – a vision that sustains life. Where there is no vision, the people perish (Prov. 29:18). This is where LOA begins. It sets the forces in play to move in the direction of the chosen aim in life. A vision requires clarity from the beginning. Clear thinking and an unwavering mental picture are prerequisites for manifesting results. Our thoughts must be on what we want, not on what we do not want. If we ask, then believe – we receive.

Mandy presents additional ideas for the LOA. It is sufficient, oftentimes, to hold a strong mental image of the desired outcome. A mental image of a wish or intent expressed while in an intense emotional state of mind is a powerful trigger of the LOA into manifestation. Recently, this happened for me in a relationship. I had almost given up on having a loving relationship. Then it happened, I met this amazing person, Jerrilyn Jarou. She is now the love of my life. This creation is truly more than I could have imagined. In this situation, my mind did not ask, my heart or soul knew what I wanted.

The prophet Habakkuk has described the LOA in the book named after him. In *The Vision of Habakkuk*, Mandy analyzes the prophet's early view on how the LOA manifests. He reveals to us the different concepts that contribute to the application of the LOA. He uses biblical stories, personal observations and anecdotes, as well as biblical verses that support his case. He presents his case in a way that allows the reader to see the simplicity of the LOA. It is not mystical, it is a human behavioral trait that is always in effect and we must direct it on our behalf to create the life we want. There cannot be "double-mindedness." We need our vision, write it down, be patient – wait for it, and emotionalize the vision at the same time living in faith.

This study of the LOA gives insight from a point of view that all of us trust, can enjoy and utilize.

Chuck Dodge, *DTM*
Making the Connection, Spirit, Mind, Body

CHAPTER ONE

THE LAW OF ATTRACTION
IN THE HOLY BIBLE

The book you are reading is intended for you – the reader and student of the Holy Bible who wants to make the Law of Attraction work for you. If you believe that the Holy Bible is a repository of the collective wisdom of the ages, then the Law of Attraction is available all in the Bible; in its entirety.

The Holy Bible consists of the Hebrew Bible and the New Testament. It is an inspired anthology of writings by many authors over millennia, probably beginning 2800 years ago. The Old Testament is a Christian term denoting the Hebrew Bible that is the holy scripture of the Jewish faith. During the last twenty-three centuries, individuals, theologians of all faiths, scribes, scholars, translators, and committees of editors did their inspired best to write, edit, translate and re-translate the Holy Scriptures, as we know them today. For me the Bible is a great repository of the best of the collective human wisdom. Now think about it – if the Law of Attraction is as powerful and as compelling as its various proponents and teachers claim it to be, then it had to be present in the stories and life-lessons canonized in the Holy Bible.

Indeed, I find a wealth of evidence for the presence of the Law of Attraction in the Holy Bible.

In the last 150 years, a movement consisting of thinkers, teachers and authors who were labeled under different names emerged to describe a phenomenon they called the Law of Attraction (LOA). A book titled *Thoughts Are Things* was published in 1889.[1] Modern time authors who dealt with the Law of Attraction described it as a rediscovered development in human thought. Today there are countless legends in the form of reports, books, and movies, as well as live classes that were written, produced and published, explaining the LOA phenomenon. The LOA in practice advises people to choose their thoughts carefully because built-in dynamic forces of thought in the human mind stir and drive the thinking person toward manifesting the thoughts into reality. Some authors described the LOA as a modern development, as if they were surprised by its existence. Still others referred to it as a secret waiting to be revealed by them to the world. Post-modern authors try to leave the impression that the LOA is somehow an innovation, impressively associated with the science called, "quantum physics." The LOA preceded the field of quantum physics by

1 Prentice Mulford (1834-1891).

millennia. New age and new thought terms such as "energy" or "vibrations" are not mentioned in the Bible. Nonetheless the actual practice and effects of the LOA are vividly described there. If anything, it is the information age that drew attention and publicized the Law of Attraction that was laying there since the Bible was written and canonized. For the Law of Attraction to be described in the Bible – its existence must have preceded the authors of the Bible.

WHAT IS THE LAW OF ATTRACTION

> *Key Concept:*
>
> *Thinkers are co-creators of their reality.*

The aphorism, *thoughts become things,* has its early origins in one form or another in the Holy Bible. Both the Hebrew Bible and the New Testament tell this same pearl of wisdom by the ancient sages in similar language. The biblical wisdom precedes the modern teachers of the LOA by over two millennia. This book describes a brief survey of selected illustrative verses, statements and stories of the LOA as told in the Bible.

Several explanations were proposed to account for the phenomenon of the LOA. The essence of the process is that, *a thought once sparked in the human mind, starts thinking about itself.* In due course, the thought spawns collateral thoughts and associated thoughts (known also as "associations"). Next, the new collateral and associative thoughts spread throughout the mind as a ripple around the original thought. The ripples of thoughts expand our consciousness to include the target idea that we wish to manifest in our reality.

The human brain has within its organ system anatomy a framework of connected neuronal circuits that is called the reticular activating system. This neuronal network is believed to mediate shifts from relaxed awareness to intensified attentive interest. Blood flow is increased in the areas of the midbrain reticular formation during performance of tasks requiring increased alertness. The increase in blood flow is believed to be a marker of increased neuronal activity. The increase in blood flow is presumed by scientists to be an indication of heightened alertness and awareness.

In addition, neuroscientists described in the last years another brain system that has been called the brain's default mode network. This default mode network is always active, even at sleep, busily processing memories, information or day-dreaming. It is thought that this neuronal default network is coordinating other parts of the brain readying it to get its tasks accomplished in alignment with the person's conscious objectives and intent.

Be it as it may, our consciousness expands, we start to see new possibilities – we conceive of questions to ask and actions to take. We make synchronous associations with various concurrent events. We seemingly start to receive invitations to participate in related events, or even to receive our desired wish or object. Even a better outcome may be delivered to us. Thus, we become co-creators of our reality as the new reality starts to manifest and take shape around us.

Repeated thinking and vivid imagination of a desired (or undesired), situation will eventually and inevitably manifest in the personal reality of the thinker.

The teachers of the LOA claim that it is this phenomenon that matches our thoughts to corresponding reality, in alignment with the original thought.

Various "tools" were suggested on how to manifest thoughts into our reality. One common tool is practicing the mental sequence of: Ask, Believe, Receive. In that case the petitioner asks for a desired condition, or declares an intention to be or have an object. The petitioner maintains a state of belief that the objective is being fulfilled by his or her readiness to receive the desired outcome.

Other tools of related nature include repeated prayers for a desired condition; writing down the desired outcome as a goal; emotionally imagining the desired outcome in the mind's eye associated with arousing excitement. Certain present day authors suggest that declaring an intention with sincere willingness to act, is sufficient to bring about the desired outcome.

DECLARING AN INTENT OR OBJECTIVE

The first occurrence, in which an idea was pronounced in a declarative format and was instantly manifested, is found right at the beginning in Genesis 1:3.[2] A divine idea was expressed – *let there be light.* And there was light. The course of creation continued for six days through manifesting divine ideas into empiric reality. Genesis 1:26-27, describes this process for the creation of humans. I am not interested here one way or another or favor any mechanism of creation (i.e., creation vs. evolution). I just indicate that an idea and its subsequent declared utterance can manifest into a reality that is perceived empirically by human beings. Note that after the first manifestation by

2 All Bible quotes are from the King James Version of the Holy Bible.

declaration, subsequent declarations of intent by the Divine were followed by an action verb. In the case of creating "a man" the biblical text says: "Let us *make* man."[3] The verb *making* indicates certain action that was taken. The lesson we learn here is that creation very often requires some form of doing to be exercised by the creator.

Another example is found in the gospels.

Matthew 7:7 and Luke 11:9 attribute to Jesus the teacher, a similar concept: *Ask and it shall be given you*. The gospels do not provide specific advice on what to ask, or instructions on how to ask. There are no limitations on how much to ask. The format is Ask, Believe, and Receive. It may be assumed that the asking is done in the form of prayer. However, prayer for that purpose is not the required tool by the gospels in this context.

---

3 Genesis 1:26.

THE VISION SUSTAINS LIFE

> *Key Concept:*
>
> *Every person must have a unique vision and purpose for life.*

The Bible is non-compromising about the need to have a personal vision for life: *Where there is no vision, the people perish:* (Prov. 29:18). People who lack a mental image for their life die. This individual mental image is a purpose or a meaning that a person gives to his or her life. This purpose becomes a goal or objective to be pursued. Where there is meaning to life – there is life. The power, forces and momentum of the LOA will go into effect and move the visionary person toward fulfillment of this objective. It is an inherent human behavioral trait.

Caution: be certain that your vision is productive, beneficial and life sustaining for yourself and for others. Visions of catastrophe are as likely to manifest to the dreamer, as are visions of benestrophe.

THINK WITH CLARITY

In the book of Proverbs, we read:
For as he thinketh in his heart, so is he:
(Prov. 23:7)

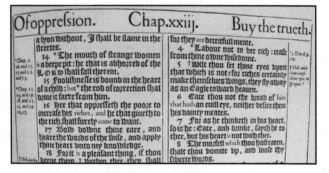

Proverbs 23:7 in a facsimile of the
King James Bible 1611.

This verse inspired the British author James Allen, known for his book (1902): *As a Man Thinketh*. In his book, Allen states that *man is literally, what he thinks, his character being the complete sum of all his thoughts*.

LESSONS FROM MODERN HISTORY

Key Concept:

The LOA provides limitless channels for manifestation

On August 28, 1963, the Reverend Martin Luther King, Jr. stood on the steps of the Lincoln Memorial in Washington, D.C. and orated his historical speech, "I Have a Dream." The speech gave the impetus for the Civil Rights Legislation by the U.S. Congress. Dr. King also said: *"I have a dream that my four little children will one day live in a nation where they will not be judged by the color of their skin, but by the content of their character."* Today, two young black girls are residing in the White House in Washington, D.C. as members of the First Family. It took the will and power of millions of Americans grouped together to make this dream a reality. While the man is gone, his vision endures and expands in present reality.

Such is the power of a visionary declaration of a dream to change a nation.

On June 12, 1987, U.S. president Ronald Reagan gave a speech at the Brandenburg Gate by the Berlin wall. In that speech President Reagan challenged Mr. Gorbachev, the General Secretary of the Communist Party of the Soviet Union: *Mr. Gorbachev, open this gate. Mr. Gorbachev, tear down this wall!"* On November 9, 1989, Berlin residents from both sides of the wall started to chip it and tear it down. It required the might of the United States people, economy and technology to change the historical reality in Europe and bring down the Berlin wall.

Such was the power of a decree made in public by one man to change the course of history.

Each oratorical declaration of vision and objective served as a trigger that ignited infinite powers that coalesced together to change history and manifest a desired outcome.

THINKERS BEWARE

The LOA operates both ways. That means it will support the manifesting of any mental picture or expressed wish. If your thoughts are negative or if you are fearful, the LOA will manifest your fears or the undesirable circumstance you are afraid of. So clear thinking and a clear, unwavering mental picture is a requirement for manifesting best results.

The biblical book of wisdom – Job, had this figured out. There Job says: *"For the thing which I greatly feared is come upon me, and that which I was afraid of is come unto me"* (Job 3:25).

Let us repeat – visions of catastrophe are as likely to manifest to the thinker, as are visions of benestrophe.

A person cannot hold two thoughts – opposite of each other and expect the thoughts to manifest. Opposite thoughts cause mental confusion and cancel each other. The LOA manifests any circumstance – whether you wish it or abhor it. Therefore, clear thinking can sometimes mean – life or death.

A joint, persistent, and repeatedly affirmed intent or goal shared by a group of friends or partners delivers powerful results. It works like a miracle for partners of two. My friends and colleagues are a married couple. For several years, they had no children. Visits with reputable fertility experts did not seem to get them closer to their aspiration of enlarging their family circle.

> *Key Concept:*
>
> *Begin where you are by acting in alignment with your goal*

After careful reflection, my friends decided to do what was under their control – expand their family by adopting a baby. They were very happy with their adopted son. In their happiness, they went ahead and adopted a second baby. Their family grew further and their joy multiplied. Shortly after that, my friend became pregnant and gave birth to a baby boy. Later she gave birth to a second boy. Altogether, they are today the proud parents of four young adult men.

My friends had a clear vision. They acted in alignment with their desires. They did what they could to manifest their desires. They did not waver. They acted in the direction of their dreams of the perfect family they envisioned. The inexplicable powers of the universe joined them to manifest their perfect vision.

> ### Key Concept:
>
> *Utilize a mastermind alliance*

Overcoming the barrier of sterility by married couples is a common goal. Manifesting an expanded family by a couple is a mastermind alliance by the married couple sharing the same goal. There are usually additional members to this mastermind alliance in the form of fertility experts and obstetricians. All are laboring as a team to manifest the joyous and precious outcome. More demonstrations of breaking the barrier of infertility come later in this chapter.

King Solomon, the author of the book of Ecclesiastes, had a mastermind alliance in mind when he wrote: *"Two are better than one; because they have a good reward for their labour"* (Eccles. 4:9).

Later he adds: *"...and a threefold cord is not quickly broken"* (Eccles. 4:12). Meaning that a mastermind group of three is a better mastermind of just two.

ATTRACTING ABUNDANCE

The LOA[4] is promoted as an instrument to bring about abundance, prosperity, or amassing wealth. Abundance and wealth can be in the form of essential supplies, provisions, property, money or lucrative objects.

Let us review a few out of numerous biblical stories of wealth manifestation.

---

4 Note that LOA is also the acronym for Law of Abundance.

The gospel of Mark illustrates the power to attract and manifest food for multitudes of people: *He had taken the five loaves and the two fishes, he looked up to heaven, and blessed, and brake the loaves, and gave them to his disciples to set before them; and the two fishes divided he among them all… And they that did eat of the loaves were about five thousand men* (Mark 6:41-44).

Note what Jesus did: *He looked up to heaven, and blessed…* This was an act of mental work that precedes or comes along with the manifestation of abundance. It may take the form of praying, meditating, envisioning, or imagining. The biblical narrative does not disclose the source of the manifested extra food. The bread could have come through many channels: donations by local residents; the gathering could have been a picnic style potluck on the northwest shore of the Lake of Galilee. A petitioner-thinker who imposes restrictions or exclusions on the sources (channels) of manifestation and abundance reduces the LOA potential for abundance.

Once a sparked thought starts to think about itself and generates collateral thoughts the LOA manifests through enhanced conscious awareness of universal abundance.

> ### Key Concept:
>
> *Let the LOA manifest for you through infinite springs of abundance*

About fifteen centuries BCE, the children of Israel, wandering in the wilderness of the Sinai desert, started to murmur (i.e., complain), against their leadership; Moses and Aaron. Their grievance was lack of sufficient food and outright hunger. A certain mental communication occurred between Moses and his deity.

Then said the Lord unto Moses, Behold, I will rain bread from heaven for you, and the people shall go out and gather a certain rate every day, that I may prove them... And the Lord spake unto Moses, saying, I have heard the murmurings of the children of Israel... And it came to pass, that at even the quails came up and covered the camp: and in the morning the dew lay round about the host. And when the dew that lay was gone up, behold upon the face of the wilderness there lay a small round thing, as small as the hoar frost on the ground. And when the children of Israel saw it they said one to another, It is manna: for they wist not what it was... (Exod. 16:1-15).

Note first, the mental activity that took place in the form of prayer. It is a revelatory communication between Moses and God – preceding the provision of food. Second, the beneficiaries received fare, some of it familiar and some was a new kind of food that they did not expect. They received quails and they received *manna*.

Once again, the LOA brings vast, boundless and infinite resolution of the state of wanting, beyond our limited human expectations.

Another case in point.

The Bible tells a story of a man, whose name was Jabez[5] (Jaabetz or phonetically reads Yaabetz in Hebrew).

He is introduced as a man who *was more honourable than his brethren*. We are told also that the family of Jaabetz made their living as – scribes[6] – they were writers. The significance of Jabez being a son to a family of scribes will be made clear later.

Jabez called on the God of Israel, blesse me indeede, and enlarge my coast, and that thine hand might bee with me and that wouldest keepe mee from evill that it may not grieve me...[7]

---

5 ιαβεσ in the Greek version of the Septuagint.

6 1 Chronicles 2:55 – And the families of the scribes which dwelt at Jabez.

7 Note the sixteenth century English spelling style. See the text in the following original folio from the KJV 1611.

Surely enough, *God granted him that which he requested.* (1 Chron. 4:9-10) It is likely that Jabez was aware of the LOA – Ask and Receive.

The Bible tells us that Jabez asked (*called on the God of Israel*), and received. The Bible does not tell what Jabez did during the time interval between Asking and Receiving. He may have taken creative action of some sort, or he may have written down his request. Jabez may have tithed, or he may have acted in the service of God. The Bible does not say that he "prayed" – it says that he just *called on the God of Israel*. We are not told that he repeated his *call* (or prayer). It is possible that he did not do anything more than get ready to receive that which he asked. The Bible does not advise us of any details. It remains the *secret* of the Bible but of a different kind.[8] In line with that possibility that Jabez did not do anymore than ask, the post-modern teachers of the LOA maintain that in order to manifest a want or a wish it may be sufficient for the person to declare intent, or set a goal, and in due course receive (achieve) it. The required condition is to *believe* that the intent, or goal,

---

8 Psalm 25:14 – *The secret of the Lord is with them that fear him; and he will shew them his covenant.*

or prayer request, is now manifested or will manifest – at its own time and on its own accord. The petitioner must stay in a mental state of heightened awareness and readiness to take inspired action, if indicated, and receive the request or petition.

What was the nature of Jabez's request? He asked for God's blessing. He asked that his territory be enlarged.[9] He asked metaphorically that "God's hand" would guide him. And he asked that he would be protected from evil.

9 The Hebrew text implies that he asked for his border to be widened. The Vulgate version reads *dilataveris terminos*. Meaning *widen the border*. It should be noted that *terminus* in English, means also a goal. In ancient Rome Terminus was the deity that presided over borders and landmarks.

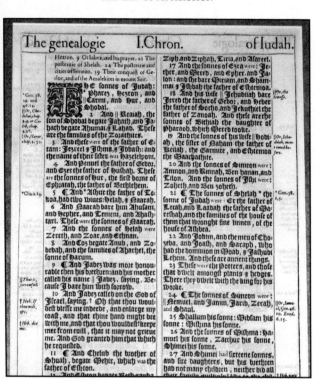

The Prayer of Jabez. 1 Chronicles 4:9-10.

From an original folio of 1611 King James Bible.

Provenance unknown.

The story of Jabez is another compelling story of the LOA in action in the Hebrew Bible. The author of Proverbs was familiar with the case history of Jabez so he concurred: *"The blessing of the Lord it maketh rich, and he addeth no sorrow with it"* (Prov. 10:22).

In plain words – success has its own justification.

A book titled, *The Prayer of Jabez,*[10] was on the New York Times #1 best seller list.

Such is the power of the LOA: a gift that keeps on giving – then and now.

THE LAW OF ATTRACTION IS AVAILABLE TO ALL

Let us move on to a different area of life where the LOA works its "miracles." The state of deep prayer or meditation is conducive to manifesting a wish, solving a specific need or satisfying a state of want.

---

10 Bruce Wilkinson. *The Prayer of Jabez.* Oregon: Multnomah Publishers, Inc., 2000.

Hannah was the wife of Elkanah. She did not bear him children. In her anguish, she went along with her husband on a pilgrimage to the temple of God in Shiloh. There in her bitterness of soul she prayed unto the Lord and wept. She asked God to remember her and give her a child. *She spoke in her heart; only her lips moved, but her voice was not heard* (1 Sam. 1:13). The priest Eli who was present there, *answered and said, Go in peace: and the God of Israel grant thee thy petition that thou hast asked of him* (1:17). By next year Hannah had a son who was named Shemuel (Samuel), meaning God hears (prayers).

This last story illustrates two points. First, it is sufficient, oftentimes, to hold a strong mental image of the desired outcome. It is not required to verbalize it loudly; nor is it necessary to write it down, although all these activities are mutually supportive. Second, a wish or intent expressed while in an intense emotional state of mind is a powerful trigger of the LOA into manifestation.

As this and other stories demonstrate, prayer while holding a mental picture of a perfect state of health facilitates healing and brings about the desired state of health and wellness.[11] In this case the state of wellness is – a fertile marital union.

In the story of Hannah and Elkanah – the prayer of supplication is a focused form of mental intent to bear children. The Bible is very clear on the nature of that intent. In the Bible that intent almost takes the form of a promise (to be fulfilled under certain conditions): *"... And I will take sickness away from the midst of thee. There shall nothing cast their young, nor be barren, in thy land"* (Exod. 23:25-26).[12]

---

11 Psalm 30:2 – *O Lord my God I cried unto thee, and thou hast healed me.*

12 The words *"cast their young,"* mean in modern English – miscarriage of pregnancy.

My friend and colleague is a physician in practice. He is a Muslim who is married. The couple had no children. After about two years into the marriage, the couple embarked on a pilgrimage to Mecca. They pursued the Muslim tradition and rituals. They returned home after one month. His head was shaven of hair. Nine months later my friend's wife gave birth to *a triplet* – two girls and a boy who are now six years old.

Abundance means prosperity in all areas of life – material riches and generations of offspring. The LOA does not discriminate between persons of different creeds.

Key Concept:

The LOA does not discriminate – it is an equal opportunity provider

---

When I was required by my health insurance carrier to select a primary care physician, guess whom I chose as my physician?

I regard with great esteem people who demonstrate in their own life the Law of Attraction. I gravitate toward these folks because they radiate a charisma of irresistible success.

CHAPTER TWO

ATTRACTING HEALTH
THROUGH THE
LAW OF ATTRACTION
IN THE HOLY BIBLE

INTRODUCTION TO ATTRACTING HEALTH

Good health can be attracted. Healing can be gained by a sick person who desires recovery and wellness. The Bible has numerous stories involving prophets and visionaries providing demonstrations of healing and recovery from diseases.

Ask any healthcare professional and she or he will agree that the first requirement for medical recovery is the patient's will to heal. Furthermore, the patient must have a will to survive. The journey to heal may be long and painful for the patient. That means holding the vision of healing with unshakable faith for long periods of time.

The LOA fundamentals for manifesting health include:

- A *will* to enjoy good health – an intention to live healthy
- A *vision* – a mental picture of good health in the mind's eye of the patient
- A support system for healing and

rehabilitation – that is a *mastermind alliance* of the patient and her or his health team.

The health team may include any or all the following:

– world-class doctors

– specialty-consultants for a second opinion

– nurses

– pastoral care practitioners

– prayer groups

Lastly, the patient must bear an unshakeable belief that the cure is on the way!

The majority of these elements are involved in most cases of a successful medical recovery and cure. As a rule the more complicated the patient's medical condition is, the greater the requirement for the visible presence of the typical elements (see Key Concepts), of the LOA. As a case in point; a healthcare provider cannot help a patient with cancer experience a remission or a cure if the patient does not want treatment.

In the previous pages, several elements of the LOA were listed and discussed and regardless of the current mainstream clinical terminology – all those elements in whatever terms the reader selects to use – must be present to effect a remission or cure. The professional jargon is not the critical element. The mental state of awareness of the patient is instrumental. The patient's ability to incorporate elements of the LOA into the plan of care that are conducive toward healing is what counts. When the right mental attitude is present, then action follows.

Let it be clear – first class healthcare providers, world-class healthcare facilities, and cutting edge medicines are solid, required components of the framework of LOA when it is applied to attracting health.

ENVISIONING THE CURE

The Bible goes back to the first Hebrew prophet and law-giver – Moses, (1,300 BCE?), and describes a case of a mass poisoning from desert snake bites. There are some recognizable elements of the LOA that were utilized to heal the sick. The snake-bite victims came to Moses their leader, "asking" him to pray for their recovery. *And Moses prayed for the people* – at their asking. (Num. 21:7).

"And Moses made a serpent of brass, and put it upon a pole, and it came to pass that if a serpent had bitten a man, when he beheld the serpent of brass, he lived" (Num. 21:9).

When we look for the elements of the LOA in this biblical story, we find first that the patients came to Moses, the healer, "asking" for help – medical help. Second, Moses prayed. Prayer of intercession is a demonstration of deliberate thinking with intent. Moses directed the patients to view and envision the venomous cause of their poisoning hung on a pole. Once they viewed the cause of their ailment, they were able to manifest their recovery. What is missing from

the story is how the serpents were later exterminated…
This item remains the secret of the Bible.

Better yet, the use of a serpent hanging from a pole
remains customary in our present times as the symbol
for the medical profession – the Aesculapius. Again,
success is its own justification…

How do patients heal and recover is not always
known in every case, even to contemporary medical
scientists. In this era of genomic medicine and gene
therapy, there are still many disease entities that
remain without cure. Nonetheless, there is something
built within the human organism that enhances its
spontaneous healing in many instances. See the case
of seasonal influenza outbreaks that come and go
annually. The influenza virus bypasses many folks
while still other folks who contract the virus, recover
on their own (or with the help of chicken soup). This
last comment is to introduce the statement in Exodus
15:26 *"…for I am the Lord that healeth thee."* If that

is the case then there is a positive role for prayer to the Divine to facilitate or enhance the process of healing. Furthermore, the LOA as we now know acts smoother and faster under the influence of a decree or a declared intent to recover by the patient.

There is a popular belief that the healing and recovery comes from the Divine, and the healers of the various occupational classes – physicians, nurses, and pastors are only channels to bring about the healing and recovery.

The legendary prophet Elijah performed two manifestations back to back: first, he demonstrated abundance. Next, he manifested healing (resurrection from death). Elijah is thought to have lived in the ninth century BCE. He is revered by the three great monotheistic religions. Elements of the LOA in action are found in both episodes that are described in 1 Kings chapter 17. The manifestation of abundance (1 Kings 17:10-16) comes first.

Next is the manifestation of healing and recovery by Elijah:

> "*...the son of the woman, the mistress of the house, fell sick; and his sickness was so sore that there was no breath left in him. ... And he said unto her, Give me thy son. And he took him out of her bosom, and carried him up into a loft, where he abode, and laid him upon his own bed. And he cried unto the Lord and said, O Lord my God, hast thou also brought evil upon the widow with whom I sojourn by slaying her son? And he stretched himself upon the child three times, and cried unto the Lord, and said, O Lord my god I pray thee let this child's soul come into him again. And the Lord heard the voice of Elijah and the soul of the child came into him again and he revived...*" (1 Kings 17:17-24)

There are three Key Concepts of the LOA that are demonstrated in this biblical story.

- First, Elijah said an intercessory prayer. Prayer is "asking!"
- Second, Elijah took action – a remedial action, a healing action.

- Third, Elijah started to work on his "case" before offering a prayer and before he had any promise from God. Elijah started to heal the child based on his belief that the child will recover. He started what seems to be CPR first and dealt with the formality of prayer later!

Lastly, the widow "received" her revived child.

PRAYER, LAW OF ATTRACTION, AND HEALING

Prayer is an integral component in the toolbox of the practice of the LOA. Prayer works when the LOA is invoked for manifesting abundance, accomplishing a successful venture, or going safely on uncharted travels. Prayer is defined as a communion with God or object of worship in a form of petition or entreaty. The person praying can pray for him or herself and can pray an intercessory prayer on behalf of another person. It is clear from the definition that prayer is said with a clear outcome in mind.

Dr. Larry Dossey in his book, *Healing Words: The Power of Prayer and The Practice of Medicine,*[13] writes: *"Prayer says something incalculably important about who we are and what our destiny may be."*[14]

Prayer for healing and recovery sets a destiny. In this case, the destiny is healing, recovery and a cure. Prayer of petition is the "ask" element of the Key Concepts of the LOA. Prayer of intercession also has an "ask" element that is combined with a "mastermind alliance" component.

As we are told, Jesus manifested abundance. Yet Jesus was also a healer. Let us review the case of the healing in Nain. The story unfolds in the gospel of Luke:

---

13 Published by HarperSanFrancisco (HarperCollins Publishers), 1993.

14 P. 6. Italics in original.

*"And it came to pass the day after, that he
went into a city called Nain; ... when he came
nigh to the gate of the city, behold, there
was a dead man carried out, the only son of
his mother, and she was a widow: and much
people of the city was with her. And when
the Lord saw her, he had compassion on her,
and said unto her, Weep not. And he came
and touched the bier: and they that bare him
stood still. And he said, Young man, I say
unto thee, Arise.*

*And he that was dead sat up, and began to
speak. And he delivered him to his mother.
And there came a fear on all and they
glorified God..."* (Luke 7:11-17).

The story as told relates that Jesus healed or
brought the dead man into life by speaking, and
ordering him—Arise. We can speculate if indeed the
man was dead. Was he just obtunded? In a coma? In
catatonic paralysis? Hysterical? He could have been
in any motionless state and was startled by the order –
Arise, and by the entourage of spectators. The point is
that there was an act of decree, the patient responded
favorably to the order, sat up, spoke and was "delivered"
back to his mother.

WHY DO GREAT BIBLICAL HEALERS
GET SICK AND DIE?

Can't great biblical healers keep on attracting their own health and longevity indefinitely?

The answer is no, they cannot as we well know from experience. They do not live forever. They do not manifest indefinitely. As humans, they have some shortcomings or internal conflicts that at a point in their life sets them up to fail, and they die under unforeseen circumstances. This book is not a treatise about theology. Nor is this a discussion on morals. Moses was denied his objective to reach in person the Land of Canaan allegedly because of certain trespasses he made against his deity. He died of old age outside his Promised Land. The Bible does not tell us how Elijah died. Jesus who died on the cross provided a wise answer to a somewhat similar question. The question was asked of Jesus when he passed by a man, blind from birth: "Master, who did sin, this man or his parents?" The answer was that neither the blind man nor his parents sinned. *"But that the works of God should be made manifest in him"* (John 9:3). In plain words, that is the way it is. Some facts of life should be left alone and need neither reason nor value judgment.

CHAPTER THREE

THE BEST PRACTICE OF
THE LAW OF ATTRACTION
IN THE HOLY BIBLE

LAW OF ATTRACTION MADE SIMPLE

In this chapter, we study the vision of the biblical prophet Habakkuk. We see how the prophet set his vision into an action plan. The prophet tells us of the valuable elements of the action plan leading from thought, through vision, to a written statement, and with excitement – to reality. Most importantly as students of the Bible, we are taught and learn from the biblical prophet the mind-set and mental awareness that transforms vision into the empiric reality of life.

In a small book in the Hebrew Bible, we find a description on how the LOA was practiced by the sages of the biblical era in order to achieve their desired results.

The biblical prophet Habakkuk lived in Jerusalem. Habakkuk is thought to have been a "staff prophet" in the temple in Jerusalem. He probably wrote his book at about the seventh century BCE (609-598 BCE?). He may have been a musician in the temple. Supporting this idea is the third chapter in the book of Habakkuk that is thought to be a misplaced Psalm.[15]

The prophet Habakkuk was no plain musician. He was a visionary, a critical thinker, and a great one at that. He did not hesitate to express his impatience with God.[16] Nonetheless, the editors of the Bible retained his criticism in the canon.

Habakkuk outlined an action plan that is inclusive and constitutes the best practice of the LOA in the bible.

Habakkuk writes in the book named after him (Hab. 2:1-4):

(Quote)

1. *I will stand upon my watch, & set mee upon the towere and will watch to see what he will say unto me and what I shall answere when I am reproved.*

---

15 Based on the word "*Shigionoth*" in Habakkuk 3:1, which is a term found only once in Psalms. *Segu* in Acadian means a lamentation.

16 Habakkuk 1:1-3.

2. *And the Lord answered me, and said,*
    Write the vision, and make it plaine upon
    tables that he may runne that readeth it.

3. *For the vision is yet for an appointed*
    time, but at the end, it shall speak,
    and not lie: though it tarry, wait for it;
    because it will surely come, it will not
    tarry.

4. *Behold, his soul, which is lifted up, is not*
    upright in him: but the just shall live by
    his faith.

(End of quote).

A facsimile of Habakkuk 2:1-4 of the King James Bible 1611. Note the sixteenth century English spelling style.

THE BEST PRACTICE OF THE LOA IN THE BIBLE

The four verses from the book of Habakkuk are the best practice advice that the Bible offers when it comes to aligning the reader's mind-set, mood and actions in order to manifest the desired outcome.

COMMENTARY:

First verse, tells the person who is seeking to manifest that he or she has to maintain a state of an open mind.

The prophet settles on top of a lofty place – a tower. The vistas from lofty places, such as towers or mountaintops, always inspire us – the observers. The prophet is a visionary person who watches his internal dialogue. The internal dialogue transpires in the form of an inner voice in the mind's ear. The prophet *lets his thought think about itself* and he watches (tunes into) collateral thoughts and associated thoughts as they appear in his awareness. This is the meaning of the first verse as it reads: *watch to see what he will say unto me...* "He" (the Divine), will spark ideas in the mind –

originating out of the mind's hidden immeasurable stores of infinite knowledge. These ideas must be given deliberate attention. In these ideas are found the visionary-thinker's prompts for inspired action. Divinity tells by implication that the visionary thinker has to listen with the mind's ear to what he is about to hear. The explicit action verbs are *set, watch, see* and *answer*. Plenty of mental heavy lifting. It seems that the prophet prepares himself for what we call a brainstorming session with the Lord.

Second verse is a directive to practice the next action item – write: *Write the vision, and make it plain upon tables that he may run that readeth it.* Wow.

Let us recap. First, there was a vision.

The Prophet had a vision! So are you: you have to have a vision.

Recall Proverbs 29:18 – *Where there is no vision, the people perish!*

You can have a vision only for your life. You cannot hold a vision for another person's life. The vision is about a future event. A vision is not about the past or about the present. The vision must be preserved by writing it down.[17]

Then comes a significant action item:

Write down the vision.

My favorite prophet Habakkuk did not have papyri and parchment nor did he have a plume and ink so his writings were inscribed on clay tablets. The vision, the goal, the intent, the idea must be preserved in writing. When a goal is committed to a written medium, it can and should be revisited – reread, studied and memorized. The goal (or intent or vision), has to be written in clear language. The expected outcome must be easy "to run" while reading it, i.e., quickly read. Present day self-improvement gurus coach us incessantly to write down our personal vision statement and goals for ourselves in the present tense, as if the goal is already manifested.

---

17 A vision may be preserved by drawing it. Albeit, the Hebrew Bible forbids drawing of human icons.

Did you ever hear a promise for freebies to be given to you by an eager silky talking salesperson and you – listened skeptically?

What did you tell the salesperson?

"I want it in writing."

When you were sitting in a job interview and the recruiter mentioned future benefits in addition to the base salary, what was your response?

"Give it to me in writing."

> ### Key Concept:
>
> *Keep writing your vision and goals*

The biblical insistence on writing things appears also in Psalms 45:1-2.

> *"My heart is inditing a good matter: I speak of the things which I have made touching the king: my tongue is the pen of a ready writer. Thou art fairer than the children of men: grace is poured into thy lips: therefore God hath blessed thee forever."*

The Psalmist suggests that expressing ("*inditing[18]*") a heart-felt sensation of *a good matter* is the target of *the pen of a ready writer.* And the outcome is: *"… therefore God hath blessed thee forever."* It is graceful to speak of a good intention – *a good matter* – but it is ways better to write it down using *the pen of a ready writer.* In alignment with this advice, we write and send personalized greeting cards for the birthdays and anniversaries of our loved ones.[19] If you do that – if you write down your *good matter* feelings of your heart – God will bless *thee* forever. Amen.

---

18 Means to compose or write as a poem.

19 The LOA is a gift that keeps on giving - Hallmark Corp. is the largest maker of greeting cards. It operates over 41,000 retail outlets in the U.S. Its revenue in 2008 was $4.3 Billion.

Use your prophetic power – send your family and friends well-wishing or get-well cards as the case may be. Declare them fortunate declare them healed.

Amazing grace!

In the first chapter we encountered an adept master of manifesting – Jabez. The Bible gives us a clue to Jabez's profession: he was the member of a large family of scribes that dwelt in the town of Jabez.[20] As a scribe, it may well have been his habit to write down his wishes and supplications. Keeping a prosperity and health journal is fashionable today.[21] It makes you write (indite) good matters and aspirations aimed to your own well being.

---

20 1 Chronicles 2:55.

21 H.A. Klauser. *Write It down, Make It Happen. Knowing What You Want And Getting it.* A Touchstone Book. Simon & Schuster, 2000.

Back to Habakkuk.

Third verse of the vision of Habakkuk addresses the element of time: *the vision is yet for an appointed time,... wait for it; because it will surely come.* Goals, intents and petitions seldom manifest instantaneously. However, the majority of goals, intents and petitions (the "asking" phase) are manifested ("given") only after a time interval between the request and the delivery ("giving" phase). Further, some inspired action may be required by the petitioner during this waiting time interval. The prophet instructs his students and listeners to wait patiently because the manifested goal *will surely come.*

Actually, an awaiting period is also a cooling period. It gives you an opportunity to reconsider your wish or maybe even change your mind...

Fourth verse has two parts.

... his soul which is lifted up, is not upright in him.

This part refers to being in an emotionally excited state – the soul which is uplifted while envisioning the goal or intent. It is mentioned above that an emotionally excited state facilitates the manifestation of the desired result. If we are not upright – if we have mixed feelings – doubts (about the desired outcome) will cause a delay in manifestation and the "giving" phase will tarry – be tardy.

Key Concept:

The just shall live by his faith

Belief. The second part of the fourth verse – *but the just shall live by his faith* – is a key to successful manifestation. Wait, believe, have faith, and live as if the delivery of your goal is already an accomplished manifestation.

Living *with* faith and living *in* faith cannot be overemphasized. Living in faith is forward looking. Living in faith is the theological touchstone of all great religions.

ATTRACTING THE PRESIDENCY

Ronald Reagan attracted to himself the presidency of the United States by using the LOA. His book title says it all: *Reagan in His Own Hand: The Writings of Ronald Reagan That Reveal His Revolutionary Vision of America.*[22] This book narrates through eyewitnesses and using original Reagan written material tells how between the years 1975-1979, Reagan *wrote* in his own hand, (no speech writer, and no ghost writer) a total of 670 radio speeches. In these radio addresses he repeatedly communicated his *vision* for the United States of America.

Get it – future president Ronald Reagan had a *vision* for himself and for America. He wrote his vision down and he communicated his vision in his speeches and addresses for four years, hundreds and hundreds of times. Then in 1979, he did something about it: he formed a mastermind alliance (known as the Reagan

22 Ronald Reagan, Annelise Anderson, George P. Shultz and Martin Anderson. *Reagan In His Own Hand: The Writings of Ronald Reagan That Reveal His Revolutionary Vision of America.* Free Press, 2001.

for President, Election Campaign Committee), when he officially ran for the presidential primaries. He won the nomination. In 1980, he was elected as president of the United States. Reagan employed five Key Concepts of the LOA: having a vision, writing the vision down hundreds of times, proclaiming the vision to the public, recruiting a mastermind alliance and taking inspired actions.

LAW OF ATTRACTION MADE SIMPLE

Once a vision is conceived there is no way back – the vision will manifest.

The expert teacher of the LOA in the book of Proverbs asserted it resolutely:

"For surely there is an end; and thine expectation shall not be cut off" (Prov. 23:18).

No "ifs" and no "buts."

Your vision is like an arrow shot out of a bow that is fulfilled – hitting its target – your expectation shall not be cut off. The expectation shall not be cut off – it cannot be canceled. *Thine* (your) expectation is destined to manifest because your expectation is your thought and your thought thinks about itself and compounds itself growing in your mind. Gradually your awareness expands and you see evidence for your thought around you. When you see the evidence, you believe that your own thought is manifesting. As you believe your own eyes and ears *"thine expectation shall not be cut off."*

A FLIGHT PLAN FOR YOUR LIFE

Every pilot is required prior to takeoff to file a flight plan with the local air traffic control tower. Commercial pilots refer to it as "completing the paperwork" prior to getting permission for takeoff. The pilot-captain of the aircraft states in writing the flight destination, the flight distance, course and the expected airspeed. The captain and first officer may say a safe trip prayer.

The flight course is subject to midflight corrections. That is obvious. The winds change direction and speed; a passenger may develop an emergency. Nonetheless the aircraft with rare exceptions lands at its destination.

The prophet Isaiah had an allegoric simile in mind when he suggested, *"they that wait upon the Lord shall renew their strength; they shall mount up with wings as eagles;"* Isaiah 40:31.

Do you have a written flight plan for your life?

You owe one to yourself.

Key Concept:

The Law of Attraction is a gift that keeps on giving

The Vision Of Habakkuk

CONCLUSION

The LOA attraction was known to the authors and editors of the Holy Bible. Humankind knew the essential elements that pertain to the function of the LOA at the time when the Bible was written and later canonized. The Bible instructs on how to live a life in alignment with LOA and has a warning message for people who disregard the subtleties of the rules of the LOA.

TEN KEY CONCEPTS OF THE LAW OF ATTRACTION

- Thinkers are co-creators of their reality

- Every person must have an individual vision and a purpose for life

- The LOA provides limitless channels for manifestation

- Begin where you are by acting in alignment with your goal

- Utilize a mastermind alliance

- Let the LOA manifest for you through infinite springs of abundance

- Keep writing your vision and goals

- The Just shall live by his faith

- The LOA does not discriminate – it is an equal opportunity provider

- The LOA is a gift that keeps on giving

RECOMMENDED READING

The Holy Bible

ACKNOWLEDGEMENTS

The author consulted or quoted in the course of writing the following biblical editions:

Single folio of the KJV. London. Robert Barker. 1611.

Facsimile of KJV. 1611. Quad-centennial limited edition. Published by the Bible Museum. Goodyear, Arizona, 2009.

Holy Bible KJV. Thomas Nelson Bibles. 1994, 2003, 2005.

The New Oxford Bible. Annotated Bible with the Apocrypha. Oxford University Press. USA, 2007.

The Leningrad Codex. A Facsimile Edition. Wm B. Eerdmans Publishing Co. Grand Rapids, Michigan, 1998.

The Parallel Bible Hebrew-English Old Testament. With the Biblia Hebraica Leningradensia, and the King James Version. Hendrickson Publishers, Inc. Peabody, Massachusetts, 2003.

Online versions of the Septuagint –
http://spindleworks.com/septuagint and the Vulgate –
http://www.perseus.tufts.edu.

The TANACH. (Hebrew Bible). Koren Publishing.
Jerusalem, Israel, 2005.

STUDY GUIDE

CHAPTER ONE

- Is the LOA a psychological or a metaphysical phenomenon?

- What is the Bible's closest description of the LOA? Book____ Chapter___ Verse___

- List the "tools" the author cites that enable the LOA.

- What is a mastermind alliance?

- Does the LOA work for select persons or for all humanity?

- List three great biblical manifesters.

- What happens in the absence of a vision? Book___ Chapter___ Verse___

CHAPTER TWO

- What is required for attracting health and wellness?

- Why do spiritual leaders and prophets get sick and die like all humans?

- How can you attract health and wellness?

CHAPTER THREE

- What are the four tools the prophet Habakkuk uses to ensure LOA manifestation?

- What is Habakkuk's theological contribution to humanity?

- Who needs a flight plan?

THE KEY CONCEPTS OF LOA

- Which Key Concept is most fundamental for the LOA?

The author will send by e-mail a 101 list of thoughts, meditations and ideas that promote the attraction of health and wellness, upon request at www.visionofhabakkuk.com.

The Vision Of Habakkuk

ABOUT THE AUTHOR

MANDY (MENAHEM) LENDER lives in Michigan
and Illinois. Born in Israel, he graduated from the
Hebrew University in Jerusalem, Israel (MD degree),
and the Dominican University, River Forest, Illinois
(MBA degree). He is board certified in internal
medicine and endocrinology. Mandy volunteers his
service and time to heal and help patients lacking health
insurance in Bay City, Michigan. Mandy has studied
the Hebrew Bible since age six and still does so. He
collects Bibles. Among his collection is a facsimile
of the first printing of the King James Bible, Robert
Barker. London 1611. ("he" Bible) quad-centennial
edition published by the Bible Museum, a facsimile
of the Gutenberg Bible (1968), and a facsimile of the
Leningrad Codex (oldest surviving complete Hebrew
Bible). Mandy is completing his memoir, *Karkinos
Farm* (www.karkinosfarm.com). Mandy is available
to share his views of *The Vision of Habakkuk and the
Law of Attraction in the Bible*.

Contact him by e-mail: mandy@mandy1st.com or
through the publisher.

CHUCK DODGE is an Inspirational Speaker and Life Coach. His business is "Making The Connection, Spirit, Mind, Body." His vision: Re-ignite the Pioneering Spirit within us. It is the spirit of being a trailblazer, entrepreneur and a collaborator. Chuck is a Toastmaster of fifteen years and achieved the highest member recognition of a *Distinguished Toastmaster*. He teaches public speaking and presentation skills. Follow Chuck Dodge on Facebook or contact him: dodgeteaches@aol.com; www.chuckdodge.com.

NOTES

NOTES

**Intermedia
Publishing Group**

Publishing That Works For You

Do you need a speaker?

Do you want Mandy Lender to speak to your group or event? Then contact Larry Davis at: (623) 337-8710 or email: ldavis@intermediapr.com or use the contact form at: www.intermediapr.com.

Whether you want to purchase bulk copies of *The Vision of Habakkuk* or buy another book for a friend, get it now at: www.imprbooks.com.

If you have a book that you would like to publish, contact Terry Whalin, Publisher, at Intermedia Publishing Group, (623) 337-8710 or email: twhalin@intermediapub.com or use the contact form at: www.intermediapub.com.